EASY TOYS
TO KNIT

EASY TOYS
TO KNIT

Cute and cuddly dolls, animals and toys

Tracy Chapman

PAVILION

First published in the United Kingdom in 2015 by
Pavilion Books Company Limited
1 Gower Street
London
WC1E 6HD

ISBN 978-1-90981-594-0

A CIP catalogue record for this book is available
from the British Library.

10 9 8 7 6 5 4 3 2 1

Reproduction by Mission, Hong Kong
Printed and bound by 1010 Printing International Ltd, China

This book can be ordered direct from the publisher at
www.pavilionbooks.com

Contents

Introduction

Childhood is a magical time in our lives that should be treasured. This collection draws on my own memories, along with years of research and experience.

I was very fortunate as a child, as some of my earliest recollections centre around knitting. We would have day trips to my relatives' homes only to find my aunties rummaging excitedly through their huge stocks of yarns, deciding what to make next.

My first lessons in knitting were from my mum, who still knits to this day and who helped me enormously with this book. She patiently taught me the craft when I was a child; my very first projects included toys and dolls' clothes. From then on I was hooked. I would help Mum to sew up and stuff the various very beautiful toys that she made for the local fete, and I would proudly carry them around in my own hand-knitted bag. I spent all my free time knitting, collecting yarns, needles and patterns – something I still do!

This compilation includes a basic doll that has many guises, an elephant to cuddle, and a variety of nursery toys just the right size for tiny hands: all ready to play a part in those precious early years.

In today's busy hi-tech world, I feel that a book like this would be an ideal companion to anyone with little ones in their life. And, of course, it is a must for those who have fond memories of knitting in their own childhood. These pages contain the best of my projects from over the years; ideal gifts for babies and toddlers just learning about life.

Happy knitting!

Knitting Basics

Knitting abbreviations

alt alternate

beg begin(ning)

cm centimetre(s)

cont continue; continuing

dec decreas (e) (ing)

garter st garter stitch

in inch(es)

inc increas(e)(ing)

k knit

k2tog knit two stitches together

M1 make one stitch (pick up horizontal loop before next stitch and knit into back of it)

mm millimetre(s)

p purl

patt pattern

psso pass slipped stitch over

p2sso pass 2 slipped stitches over

rem remain(ing)

rep repeat

RS right side

sl1 slip one stitch

st(s) stitch(es)

st st stockinette stitch (US: stocking stitch)

tog together

tbl through back of loop

WS wrong side

yfwd yarn forward

yon yarn over needle

yrn yarn around needle

Knitting needle and crochet hook conversions

You should be aware that different parts of the crafting world use different sizing systems for knitting needles and crochet hooks. In this book we use both metric sizes (the measurement is in millimetres) and US sizes – the US has its own idiosyncratic system.

Knitting needles

Metric	US
2mm	0
2.25mm	1

2.75mm	2
3mm	–
3.25mm	3
3.5mm	4
3.75mm	5
4mm	6
4.5mm	7
5mm	8
5.5mm	9
6mm	10
6.5mm	10.5
7mm	–
7.5mm	11
8mm	13
10mm	15

Crochet hooks

Metric	US
2.00mm	–
2.25mm	B-1
2.50mm	–
2.75mm	C-2
3.00mm	–
3.25mm	D-3
3.50mm	E-4
3.75mm	F-5
4.00mm	G-6

US and UK knitting terms

There are some differences between knitting terminology in the UK and the US. In this book we use UK terms with US terms given in brackets. Here are the key differences to keep in mind:

UK terms	US terms
cast off	bind off
moss stitch	seed stitch
stocking stitch	stockinette stitch
tension	gauge

Knitting stitches

A reminder of some of the key knitting stitches:

Garter stitch = knit every row.
Moss stitch (US: seed stitch) = knit 1, purl 1; on the wrong-side row you purl the knit stitches and knit the purl stitches.
Stocking stitch (US: stockinette stitch) = knit on the right side; purl on the wrong side (reverse this to make reverse stocking/stockinette stitch).

Dolls and Dolls' Clothes

First of all in this section we give you a basic doll pattern (page 12). Once you have mastered this simple pattern, you can experiment with different facial expressions and hairstyles. This basic doll can be amended and adapted into the dolls shown later, such as the sailor boy (page 24) and the fairy doll (page 28).

Here you will also find a range of outfits that every child will love. Ideas include a pink ballerina costume (page 22), a traditional Japanese outfit (page 30), a rag doll's top and skirt (page 34), a winter jacket (page 38) and a floppy hat (page 41).

All the clothes are interchangeable, and fit the basic doll patterns. Once you've tried these, experiment with different colours and yarns to create your own wardrobe of clothes and give each of your toys their own distinct character.

Basic Doll

This Basic Doll pattern is the foundation for all the dolls in this book. Turn to page 16 for a selection of clothes to suit her every mood and social engagement. Then meet her friends Ballerina Belle, Artie the Sailor, Fairy Longlegs, Japanese Doll and Rag Doll.

MATERIALS

50g balls of 4ply (sport-weight) 100% cotton: 2 x pale pink or other suitable flesh colour (A), 1 x light brown or other suitable colour for hair (B) and 1 x white for knickers (C)
Black and pink embroidery thread for eyes and mouth
3mm (US: 2) needles
Toy stuffing

TENSION (GAUGE)

23 sts and 32 rows to 10cm (4in) using yarn A measured over st st on 3mm (US: 2) needles.

HEAD (make 2 pieces)

Using yarn A, cast on 21 sts.
Row 1: K.
Row 2: K1, inc in next st, p to last st, inc in next st, k1 (23 sts).
Row 3: K.
Row 4: As row 2 (25 sts).

Row 5: K.
Row 6: K1, p to last st, k1.
Cont in st st, without further shaping, for 32 rows.
Next row: K2tog twelve times, k1 (13 sts).
Next row: P.
Next row: K2tog six times, k1 (7 sts).
Cast (bind) off.

LEGS (make 2)

Using yarn A, cast on 24 sts.
Work 64 rows in st st.
Decrease as follows:
Next row: K1,* k2tog, k2, rep from * to last 3 sts, k2tog, k1 (18 sts).
Next row: P.
Next row: K1, *k2tog, k2, rep from * to last 1 st, k1 (14 sts).
Next row: P.
Next row: K1, * k2tog, k2, rep from * to last 1 st, k1.
Next row: P.
Next row: K1, * k2tog, k2, rep from * to

last 2 sts, k2 (9 sts).
Next row: P.
Break thread and draw through rem 9 sts and secure.

BODY (make 2 pieces)
Using yarn A, cast on 28 sts.
Work 36 rows in st st.
Cast (bind) off 4 sts at beg of next 4 rows (12 sts).
Cast (bind) off rem 12 sts.

ARMS (make 2)
Using yarn A, cast on 16 sts.
Work 50 rows in st st.
Cast (bind) off 4 sts at beg of next 4 rows.

TO MAKE UP BASIC DOLL
Sew in all ends. Join head pieces, using mattress stitch, and stuff firmly. Join the two body pieces in the same way and stuff. Join seams of legs, stuff firmly and attach to bottom of body. Fold and close seams on arms. Attach to main body. Attach head to complete the doll, ensuring that the neck is stuffed sufficiently to support the head.

HAIR
To make the hair using yarn B, begin at the back of neck: sew a loop, then secure with a small stitch. Continue working in this manner until the whole head is covered. Make the fringe in the same way, using shorter loops.

FEATURES
Sew the features on the face as illustrated, using black embroidery thread for the eyes and pink for the lips.

KNICKERS
Using yarn C, cast on 24 sts.
Work in k1, p1 rib for 4 rows.
Work 4 rows in st st.
Next row: Dec 1 st at each end of next and every following alt row until 10 sts remain.
Next row: K2tog to end (5 sts).
Work 3 rows in st st.
Next row: Inc in every st (10 sts).
Next row: Inc 1 st at each end of next and every following alt row until there are 24 sts.
Work 4 rows in st st.
Work in k1, p1 rib for 4 rows.
Cast (bind) off.
Fold in half and join the side seams.

Basic Wardrobe

The Basic Doll has a set of mix-and-match outfits to choose from: a wrap top, a pretty skirt with a motif around the hem, a Fair Isle jumper with a snowflake pattern, and a pair of snug trousers. Knit her the whole set and she'll always look perfectly turned out and ready for any adventure.

Wrap top

MATERIALS
50g ball of 4ply (sport-weight) 100% cotton: 1 x purple
3mm (US: 2) needles

TENSION (GAUGE)
23 sts and 32 rows to 10cm (4in) measured over st st on 3mm (US: 2) needles.

BODY
Cast on 28 sts.
Work 28 rows in st st.
Next row: K9, cast off centre 10 sts and k to end.
Working on these 9 sts only, work 2 rows in st st.
Next row: K1, p to last 1 st, k1.
Next row: K1, pick up loop before next st and knit into back of it; k to end (19 sts).
Cont increasing in this manner on the front edge until there are 28 sts.

Work 1 row.
Next row (RS facing): Cast on 31 sts and k to the end.
Cast (bind) off.
With WS of work facing, rejoin yarn to rem sts using st st.
Work 1 row.
Next row: K1, p to last st, k1.
Next row: K to last st, pick up loop before st and knit into the back of it, k1.
Rep last 2 rows and cont increasing in this manner, on the front edge only, until there are 28 sts.
Complete to match first side.
Cast (bind) off.

SLEEVES (make 2)
Cast on 22 sts.
Work 6 rows in st st.
Next row: Increase 1 st at each end of this and following 4th row until there are 26 sts.
Work 27 rows in st st.
Cast (bind) off.

Skirt pattern

■ A

☐ B

TO MAKE UP WRAP TOP

Fold sleeves in half lengthways and sew in place on top of shoulder. Join sleeve and side seams.

Striped knickers

MATERIALS

50g balls of 4ply (sport-weight) 100% cotton: 1 x purple and 1 x white

TENSION (GAUGE)

23 sts and 32 rows to 10cm (4in) measured over st st on 3mm (US: 2) needles.

Note

This version is worked in stripes, beginning with purple. Change colour on every third row. Follow instructions for Knickers on page 14.

Skirt

MATERIALS

50g balls of 4ply (sport-weight) 100% cotton: 1 x lilac (A) and 1 x white (B)
3mm (US: 2) needles
3mm (C-2/D-3) crochet hook
Small button

TENSION (GAUGE)

23 sts and 32 rows to 10cm (4in) measured over st st on 3mm (US: 2) needles.

Using yarn A, cast on 140 sts.
Work 4 rows in garter st.
Work 2 rows in st st.
Next row: Using the Fair Isle technique, set motif as illustrated in chart on page

18, using yarn B.
Cont in st st for a further 24 rows.
Decrease row.
Next row: K2, * k2tog, rep from * to last
2 sts, k2 (68 sts).
Next row: P.
Next row: K4, * k2tog, k1, rep from * to
last 4 sts, k4 (48 sts).
Work 2 rows in st st.
Cast (bind) off.

TO MAKE UP SKIRT
Darn in all ends on the skirt and join
sides by mattress stitch. Leave about
4cm (1½in) open at the top. Sew on a
small button and crochet a chain to use
as a loop.

Fair Isle jumper

MATERIALS
50g balls of DK (light worsted) cotton
and acrylic blend: 1 x cream (A) and
1 x light blue (B)
4.5mm (US: 7) needles

TENSION (GAUGE)
18 sts and 25 rows to 10cm (4in)
measured over st st on 4.5mm
(US: 7) needles.

FRONT
Using yarn A, cast on 25 sts.
Work k1, p1 rib for 4 rows.
Cont in st st for 4 rows.
Next row: Set snowflake motif as
follows, using Fair Isle technique and
chart opposite:
K6, next 13 sts follow chart, k6.
Work 13-row chart to complete motif.
Cont in yarn A only, working a further
4 rows in st st.
Work 4 rows in k1, p1 rib.
Cast (bind) off.

BACK
Work as front, omitting the motif.

SLEEVES (make 2)
Using yarn A, cast on 22 sts.
Work 6 rows in st st.
Next row: Decrease 1 st at each end of
this and every following 4th row until
there are 14 sts.
Work 1 row without shaping.
Next row: Work 4 rows of k1, p1 rib.
Cast (bind) off.

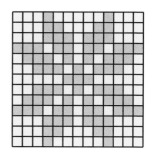

Jumper motif

☐ A

☐ B

TO MAKE UP FAIR ISLE JUMPER
As for Teddy Bear's Blue Sweater (see page 67).

Trousers

MATERIALS
50g ball of DK (light worsted) cotton and acrylic blend: 1 x light blue
4.5mm (US: 7) needles
20cm (8in) length of elastic

TENSION (GAUGE)
18 sts and 25 rows to 10cm (4in measured over st st on 4.5mm (US: 7) needles.

TROUSERS (make 2 pieces)
Cast on 25 sts.
Knit 2 rows.
Next row: Beg with a k row, work in st st for 50 rows.
Next row: Work 4 rows in k1, p1 rib.
Cast (bind) off.

TO MAKE UP TROUSERS
Darn in ends. Starting at bottom of leg, join seams using mattress stitch. Work until 4cm (1½in) from rib. Join both legs at centre seam. Sew elastic around top of trousers to form a waistband.

Ballerina Clothes

This graceful Ballerina Belle has all the right accessories to use in her exciting performances – a tutu, ballet shoes, legwarmers and even a delicate necklace!

MATERIALS

50g balls of 4ply (sport-weight) 100% cotton: 2 x pale pink (A), 1 x brown (B), 1 x white (C) and 1 x dark pink (D)
Oddments of DK (light worsted) yarn in white (E)
Black and pink embroidery thread for eyes and mouth
3mm (US: 2) needles
3mm (US: C-2/D-3) crochet hook
25cm (10in) of ballet net in light pink or white
Bias binding to match net
Press studs
2 sequins, 2 beads, embroidery cotton
Toy stuffing

TENSION (GAUGE)

23 sts and 32 rows to 10cm (4in) using yarn A measured over st st on 3mm (US: 2) needles.

DOLL

As Basic Doll (page 12) using yarn A.

HAIR

As Basic Doll (page 14) using yarn B.

KNICKERS

As for Basic Doll (page 14) using yarn C.

WRAP TOP

As for Wrap Top (page 17) using yarn D.

TUTU

Fold the ballet net in half lengthways and gently gather it to fit around the waist of the doll. Tack as you go, then sew securely. Take the bias binding and fold it over the gathered waist edge of the net. Pin and sew in place, covering the tacking stitches. To finish, sew the press stud parts to either end of the waistband. Trim the tutu to the desired length.

SHOES

Using yarn D and the crochet hook, make a foundation ring of 8 ch, join with a slip stitch and work in rounds.

Round 1: Make 2 ch; work 8tr (US: dc) into ring, working over loose end.

Round 2: As round 1.

Round 3: As round 1. Continue working in this way until shoe fits securely on the foot.

To finish, crochet two chains on either side of shoe to use as straps. Make another shoe to match.

NECKLACE

Thread two sequins, in different colours and shapes, on to a piece of embroidery cotton. Thread on a bead, then thread the cotton back through the two sequins.

LEGWARMERS (make 2)

Using yarn E, cast on 24 sts. Cont in k2, p2 rib for 40 rows. Cast (bind) off in patt.

To finish, join side seams using mattress stitch.

HAIRBAND

Using yarn D, cast on 5 sts. Work in st st until, when the hairband is slightly stretched, it fits across the top of the head.

Sailor Clothes

Watching the ships in a busy harbour inspired me to design this cheeky chap, Artie the Sailor, who is full of tall tales about his journeys around the world and encounters with monsters of the deep.

MATERIALS

50g balls of 4ply (sport-weight) 100% cotton: 1 x cream (A), 1 x navy (B) and 1 x white (C)
Black and pink embroidery thread for eyes and mouth
3mm (US: 2) needles
20cm (8in) length of elastic
Toy stuffing

TENSION (GAUGE)

23 sts and 32 rows to 10cm (4in) using yarn A measured over st st on 3mm (US: 2) needles.

DOLL

As Basic Doll (see page 12) using yarn A.

TUNIC TOP BACK

Using yarn B, cast on 28 sts.
Work in st st until the piece is 14cm (5½in) long.
Cast (bind) off.

TUNIC TOP FRONT

Using yarn B, cast on 28 sts.
Work 26 rows in st st.
Divide for neck: K14, work on these sts only.
Next row: P.
Decrease 1 st on neck edge on this and following 7 alt rows (6 sts).
Work 3 rows in st st.
Cast (bind) off.
Rejoin yarn to rem 14 sts and reverse shaping to match first side.

TUNIC INSET

Using yarn C, cast on 20 sts.
Work in st st throughout.
Work 11 rows.
Change to yarn B and knit 1 row.
Cast (bind) off.

SLEEVES (make 2)

Using yarn B, cast on 22 sts.
Work 6 rows in st st.
Next row: Increase 1 st at each end of

this and every following 4th row until there are 26 sts.
Work 20 rows in st st.
Cast (bind) off.

TROUSERS (make 2 pieces)

Using yarn B, cast on 35 sts.
Work 2 rows in garter st.
Work 74 rows in st st.
Next row: K4, * yfwd, k2tog, rep from * four times, knit to end of row.
Purl 2 rows.

Cast (bind) off.

COLLAR

Using yarn B, cast on 48 sts.
Work 4 rows in garter st, then change to yarn C.
Next row: K2tog tbl, k12, k2tog tbl, k16, k2tog, k12, k2tog (44 sts).
Row 6: K2tog, k to last 2 sts, k2tog (42 sts).
Row 7: Rejoin yarn B, k2tog tbl, k10, k2tog tbl, k14, k2tog, k10, k2tog (38 sts).

Row 8: As row 6 (36 sts).
Row 9: Rejoin yarn C, k2tog tbl, k8, k2tog tbl, k12, k2tog, k8, k2tog (32 sts).
Row 10: As row 6 (30 sts).
Break off yarn C and cont in yarn B throughout.
Row 11: K2tog tbl, k6, k2tog tbl, k10, k2tog, k6, k2tog (26 sts).
Row 12: K2tog, p to last 2 sts, k2tog (24 sts).
Row 13: K2tog tbl, k4, k2tog tbl, k8, k2tog, k4, k2tog (20 sts).
Row 14: As row 12 (18 sts).
Row 15: K2tog tbl, k2, k2tog tbl, k6, k2tog, k2, k2tog (14 sts).
Row 16: As row 12 (12 sts).
Cast (bind) off.

HAT

Using yarn B, cast on 32 sts.
Work 3 rows in garter st.
Row 4: Change to yarn C. Sl1, p to the last st, k1.
Work 2 rows in garter st.
Row 7: Sl1, k2, * increase once in the next st, k4, rep from * to the last 4 sts, increase once in the next st, k3 (38 sts).
Row 8 (and every following alt row): Sl1, p to the last st, k1.
Row 9: Sl1, k2, * increase once in the next st, k5, rep from * to the last 5 sts,

increase once in the next st, k4 (44 sts).
Row 11: Sl1, (k5, k2tog) six times, k1 (38 sts).
Row 13: Sl1, k to the end of the row.
Row 15: Sl1, (k4, k2tog) six times, k1 (32 sts).
Row 17: Sl1, (k3, k2tog) six times, k1 (26 sts).
Row 19: Sl1, (k2, k2tog) six times, k1 (20 sts).
Row 21: Sl1, (k1, k2tog) six times, k1 (14 sts).
Row 23: Sl1, (k2tog) six times, k1 (8 sts).
Break off yarn and draw through rem sts and fasten off.

TO MAKE UP SAILOR

Darn in all ends. Join seam on hat and stitch open side. Join shoulders on tunic, sew inset into position as illustrated, attach sleeves and sew side and sleeve seams using mattress stitch. Make a twisted cord and thread through eyelets. Starting at bottom of leg, join trouser seams using mattress stitch. Work until 4cm (1½in) from rib. Join both legs at centre seam. Thread needle with elastic and sew a length around top of trousers to form a waistband.

Fairy Clothes

Share magical times with enchanting Fairy Longlegs. She has delicate wings and a beautiful organza skirt that looks like gossamer.

MATERIALS

50g balls of 4ply (sport-weight) 100% cotton: 2 x cream (A), 1 x gold (B) and 1 x white (C)
Black and pink embroidery thread for eyes and mouth
3mm (US: 2) needles
3mm (US: C-2/D-3) crochet hook
50cm (19¾in) length of white organza
30cm (12in) length of bias binding tape
1m (39½in) length of narrow silver ribbon
Pins, needle and thread
Press stud
2 buttons
Toy stuffing

TENSION (GAUGE)

23 sts and 32 rows to 10cm (4in) measured over st st on 3mm (US: 2) needles.

DOLL

As Basic Doll (page 12) * using yarn A.

*LEGS

Work 84 rows (not 64 rows) in st st.

HAIR

As Basic Doll (page 14) using yarn B.

KNICKERS

As Basic Doll (page 14) using yarn C.

TOP

As Sailor Top front sections
(page 24) using yarn C.

The top is constructed by
joining the front sections on
one side, using mattress stitch.
This will be the back seam.

Fold the outside edges into the
middle and catch the shoulders
together to form a jacket. Sew
on the buttons, and crochet
two small button loops.

WINGS

Using yarn C, cast on 42 sts.
Work 36 rows in garter st.
Eyelet row: K2, * yfwd,
k2tog, rep from * to last 2 sts, k2.
This forms the holes for the ribbon to be
threaded through.
Cont in garter st for a further 18 rows.
Cast (bind) off.

Thread ribbon through the eyelet holes,
pull to gather slightly and tie ribbon
around doll's waist to form wings.

SKIRT

Fold the white organza along the width,
forming a long rectangle, and tack along
the top using running stitch. Gather the
fabric to fit around the waist of the fairy
and sew securely. Sandwich the raw edge
of the organza in between the bias binding
tape and pin, tack and sew in place. Attach
the press stud. Trim off any loose threads.
Wrap small sections of ribbon around the
ankles and sew in place.

Japanese Clothes

This pretty doll from Japan wears a brightly coloured traditional kimono and has an upswept hairstyle, decorated with blossoms. Her calm, meditative air makes her a good friend to have around, and she's the perfect confidante. She'll be a welcome guest in anyone's home.

MATERIALS

50g balls of 4ply (sport-weight) 100% cotton: 2 x cream (A), 2 x red (C), 1 x white (D) and 1 x light blue (E)
50g ball of 4ply (sport-weight) 100% wool in tweed effect: 1 x grey (B)
Black and pink embroidery thread for eyes and mouth
3mm (US: 2) needles
50cm (19¾in) length of light blue ribbon
3 mini ribbon roses
Toy stuffing

TENSION (GAUGE)

23 sts and 32 rows to 10cm (4in) using yarn A measured over st st on 3mm (US: 2) needles.

DOLL

As Basic Doll (page 12) using yarn A.

HAIR

As Basic Doll (page 14) using yarn B.

Follow instructions for long hair sections on Rag Doll (page 34), using the same technique, but only around the outer hairline. When completed, gather up at crown of head and secure with same yarn. Allow the loose ends to fall equally around the tied hair and gather up to form a bun. Sew securely and attach a rose on the side of the head at the front.

KIMONO BACK

Using yarn C, cast on 34 sts.
Knit 2 rows.
Next row: K.
Next row: K2, p to last 2 sts, k2.
Rep last 2 rows until work measures 15cm (6in).
Cont in st st, knitting first 2 and last 2 sts of every row * until work measures 27cm (10½in) from cast-on.
Shape shoulders:
Cast (bind) off 6 sts at beg of next 4 rows (10 sts).

Cast (bind) off rem 10 sts.

KIMONO FRONT
Work as Back until * (22cm/8½in).
Divide for front: K17, turn work, k1, p to last st, k1.
Cont on these 17 sts only until work measures 27cm (10½in) from cast-on.
Cast (bind) off 6 sts (11 sts).
Work 1 row.
Cast (bind) off 6 sts (5 sts).
Cast (bind) off rem 5 sts.
Rejoin yarn to rem 17 sts and work to match first side.

KIMONO SLEEVES (make 2)
Using yarn C, cast on 44 sts.
Work 6 rows in garter st.
Cont in st st until work measures 9cm (3½in).
Cast (bind) off.

TO MAKE UP KIMONO
Darn in all loose ends. Join shoulder seams using mattress stitch. Attach sleeves and join sleeve and side seams. Press work to keep open side seams flat.

KNICKERS
As Basic Doll (page 14) using yarn D.

BACK PILLOW
Using yarn E, cast on 25 sts.
Work 25 rows in st st.
Next row (RS): P 1 row to make fold.
Next row (WS): Cont in st st, starting with a p row, and work 24 rows.
Cast (bind) off.

TO MAKE UP THE BACK PILLOW
Darn in all loose ends. Fold in half and sew sides using mattress stitch. Stuff slightly and close last side. Attach ribbon to pad as illustrated.

Rag Doll Clothes

With her distinctive golden plaits and tousled fringe, Rag Doll cuts a tall, striking figure. She's happy to sit dangling her long legs over a shelf, watching everything that's going on. She's all ready for summer days in a cute sleeveless top and skirt with interesting hem detail, embellished with an embroidered daisy.

MATERIALS

50g balls of 4ply (sport-weight) 100% cotton: 2 x pale pink (A) and 1 x white (C)
50g balls of DK (light worsted) cotton and acrylic blend: 1 x yellow (B), 1 x pink (D) and 1 x lilac (E)
Black and pink embroidery thread for eyes and mouth
3mm (US: 2) and 4.5mm (US: 7) needles
3.25mm (D-3) crochet hook
Beads
Toy stuffing

TENSION (GAUGE)

For doll's body: 23 sts and 32 rows to 10cm (4in) using yarn A measured over st st on 3mm (US: 2) needles.

For doll's clothes: 18 sts and 25 rows to 10cm (4in) using yarn D measured over st st on 4.5mm (US: 7) needles.

DOLL

As Basic Doll (page 12) using yarn A and 3mm (US: 2) needles.
Legs: work an additional 20 rows for extra length.

HAIR

As Basic Doll (page 14) using yarn B. To make fringe, follow instructions for Basic Doll.

To make the longer sections of hair, cut lengths of yarn measuring 60cm (24in) and fold in half. Using a crochet hook and starting at the back of the fringe, insert hook and draw through folded end of yarn; secure by threading long ends through. Tighten up. Repeat this technique in rows across the head, working down towards the neck.

To make plaits, divide the hair into two halves and secure gently. Tidy up both sections and divide each of them into

three equal bunches. Plait down the length. Tie with yarn in a bow.

FEATURES
Using black and pink embroidery thread, darn face as illustrated.

KNICKERS
As Basic Doll (page 14) using yarn C

and 3mm (US: 2) needles.

SKIRT
Using yarn D and 4.5mm (US: 7) needles, cast on 74 sts.
Knit 1 row.
Commence pattern:
Row 1: K.
Row 2: P.

Row 3: K1, * (k2tog) three times, (yfwd, k1) six times, rep from * to last st, k1.
Row 4: K.
Rep these 4 rows once more.
With WS facing, work a further 28 rows without shaping.
Next row: K2tog to end of row (37 sts).
Work a further 6 rows in garter st.
Cast (bind) off.

TO MAKE UP THE SKIRT
Darn in all loose ends and embroider a 'lazy daisy' motif on bottom of skirt above the pattern sequence.

SLEEVELESS TOP BACK
Use yarn E and 4.5mm (US: 7) needles, cast on 25 sts.
Work 4 rows in moss st (seed st).
Work 32 rows in st st.
Cast (bind) off.

SLEEVELESS TOP FRONT
Use yarn E and 4.5mm (US: 7) needles, cast on 25 sts.
Work 4 rows in moss st (seed st).
Work 14 rows in st st.
Next row: Divide for front. K13, turn work and p to end.
Next row: K to last 2 sts, k2, turn work and p to end.

Work a further 2 rows without shaping.
Next row: Decrease 1 st at neck edge.
Rep last 3 rows until 8 sts remain.
Cast (bind) off.
Rejoin yarn to rem 12 sts and complete to match first side.

TO MAKE UP THE TOP
Darn in all loose ends. Join all seams using mattress stitch. Join shoulder and side seams.

Winter Jacket

Make this beautiful winter jacket, which fits the Basic Doll pattern (page 12), and will match nicely with the trousers (shown on page 21) or the skirt (shown on page 18).

MATERIALS
50g balls of DK (light worsted) cotton and acrylic blend: 1 x beige (A) and 1 x white (B)
4.50mm (US: 7) needles

TENSION (GAUGE)
18 sts and 25 rows to 10cm (4in) measured over st st on 4.5mm (US: 7) needles.

SPECIAL ABBREVIATION
Make loop: ML – On the right side of the work knit to the position of the loop. Knit the next stitch, but do not allow the loop to drop off the left-hand needle. Bring the yarn to the front between the two needles and wind the yarn around your left thumb.

Take the yarn to the back again between the needles and knit into the same stitch remaining on the left-hand needle – so making two stitches out of the original one. Slip the stitch off the left-hand needle.

Place both stitches back on the left-hand needle and knit them together through the back of the loops to complete the stitch.

MAIN BODY & SLEEVES (worked in one piece)
Starting at lower edge of back and using yarn A, cast on 26 sts.
Work 16 rows in st st.
Sleeve shaping:
With RS facing and working in st st throughout, cast on 3 sts at beg of next 8 rows (50 sts).
Work 8 rows without further shaping.
Neck shaping:
K21, cast (bind) off centre 8 sts, k to end.
Working on first set of 21 sts only, and beg with a p row, work 7 rows in st st.

Next row (RS) (neck edge): Cast on 4 sts, k to end (25 sts).

Next row (WS): Cast (bind) off 3 sts at sleeve edge on next and three following alt rows (13 sts).

Next row (RS): Beg with a k row, work 16 rows in st st.

Cast (bind) off.

With WS facing, rejoin yarn to rem 21 sts. Beg with a p row, work 6 rows in st st.

Next row (WS) (neck edge): Cast on 4 sts, p to end.

Next row (RS): Cast (bind) off 3 sts at sleeve edge on the next and 3 following alt rows (13 sts).

Beg with a p row, work 16 rows in st st. Cast (bind) off.

HOOD

Using yarn B, cast on 43 sts.

Row 1: K1, *ML, k1, rep from * to end.

Row 2: Purl.

Row 3: As row 1.

Row 4: Change to yarn B and purl.

Next row (RS): Beg with a k row, cont in st st until work measures 6cm (2½in) from cast-on.

Cast (bind) off.

MAKING UP

Darn in all loose ends. Fold hood in half with loops at the front, join back seam (cast-off/bound-off edge) together by using mattress stitch. Attach to main body of jacket easing the side edges around neck shaping. Starting at a cuff, join sleeve seams in the same manner leaving a 3cm (1¼in) vent at the bottom of the side edges.

Make two twisted cords each measuring 15cm (6in) and attach to jacket at the bottom of the hood on the neck edge.

Floppy Brimmed Hat

This gorgeous floppy hat is perfect for a lazy day in the sunshine. It can be knitted in any colour to go with the outfit you make for any of the dolls in the book. Here it is modelled by the ballerina doll, but it could work equally well on the rag doll or the basic doll.

MATERIALS
50g ball of DK (light worsted) cotton and acrylic blend: 1 x ecru
4.50mm (US: 7) needles

TENSION (GAUGE)
18 sts and 25 rows to 10cm (4in) measured over st st on 4.5mm (US: 7) needles.

CROWN
Cast on 40 sts.
Work 6 rows in st st.
Shape crown:
Row 7: * (K6, k2tog) rep from * to end (35 sts).
Row 8: Purl.
Row 9: * (K5, k2tog) rep from * to end (30 sts).
Row 10: Purl.
Row 11: * (K4, k2tog) rep from * to end (25 sts).
Row 12: Purl.

Row 13: * (K3, k2tog) rep from * to end (20 sts).
Row 14: Purl.
Row 15: * (K2, k2tog) rep from * to end (15 sts).

Row 16: Purl.
Row 17: * (K1, k2tog) rep from * to end (10 sts).
Row 18: Purl.
Break yarn and draw through rem 10 sts and secure.

BRIM
With RS facing, pick up and knit 40 sts along cast-on edge of crown.
Row 2 (WS): Inc in every st (80 sts).
Row 3 (RS): * K3, inc 1, rep from * to end (100 sts).
Row 4: Purl.
Row 5: Knit.
Row 6: Purl.

Row 7: * K4, inc 1, rep from * to end (120 sts).
Row 8: Purl.
Row 9: Knit.
Row 10: Purl.
Row 11 (eyelet row): K2, *yfwd, k2tog, rep from * to end.
Row 12: Purl.
Row 13: Knit.
Row 14: Purl.
Cast (bind) off.

MAKING UP
Darn in all loose ends.
To complete frilly edge, fold along eyelet row and slip stitch into place. Join seam by using mattress stitch.

Animals

The animals in this section are ideal to knit for children and adults alike and would make great gifts. Take a look at the cheeky monkey or the solemn penguin. Each has its own character and style that will shine through when you make it. The only problem will be in deciding who to make first. Mousie Mousie is so cute, who could resist him! Robbie the Fish and Mr Bumble would be loved by a baby or toddler, while Rabbit and Kangaroo would suit an older child or adult. Reggie the Snake would make anyone laugh and Teddy Bear and Loulou the Elephant are great for hugs. The choice is yours.

Tucker the Monkey

This appealing little monkey, with a heart-shaped face, is full of charm. He's curious about life and dressed for adventure in a snazzy waistcoat and scarf. Tucker is full of mischief and great fun to have around.

MATERIALS

50g balls of 4ply (sport-weight) 100% wool yarn with tweed effect:
4 x brown (A; use yarn doubled apart from ears), 1 x fawn (B) and 1 x red (D; use yarn doubled)
50g ball of DK (light worsted) 100% wool yarn with tweed effect: 1 x lime green (C)
Black embroidery thread for eyes, nose and mouth
3mm (US: 2) needles
2 x 3mm (US: 2) double-pointed needles
Toy stuffing

TENSION (GAUGE)

28 sts and 40 rows to 10cm (4in) using yarn A (single) measured over st st on 3mm (US: 2) needles.

BODY – BACK

Using yarn A doubled, cast on 12 sts.
Work 2 rows in st st.
Next row: Increase 1 st at each end of this and every following 4th row until there are 20 sts.
Work 26 rows without shaping.
Shape top of body back:
Decrease 1 st at each end of next and every following alt row until there are 6 sts.
Work 1 row.
Cast (bind) off.

BODY – FRONT (2 PIECES)

SIDE 1

Using yarn A doubled, cast on 6 sts.
Work 2 rows in st st.
Next row: Increase 1 st at each end of this and every following 4th row until there are 12 sts.
Work 26 rows without further shaping **.
Next row: With RS facing, decrease 1 st at end of next row and at end of every following 4th row until there are 8 sts.
Work 1 row.
Next row: Decrease 1 st at each end of this and every following alt row until 2 sts remain.

Cast (bind) off.

SIDE 2
Work as side 1 until **.
Decrease at beg of next row and beg of every following 4th row until there are 8 sts.
Work 1 row.
Next row: Decrease 1 st at each end of this and every following alt row until there are 2 sts.
Cast (bind) off.

LEGS (make 2)
Using yarn A doubled, cast on 20 sts.
Working in st st, cont until work measures 20cm (8in) (approx. 70 rows).
Cast (bind) off.

ARMS
Using yarn A doubled, cast on 16 sts.
Working in st st, cont until work measures 16cm (6¼in) (approx. 56 rows).
Shape top of arm:
Next row: K1, k2tog, k4, k2tog, k4, k2tog, k1 (13 sts).
Next row: Purl.
Next row: K1, k2tog, k7, k2tog, k1 (11 sts).
Next row: Purl.
Next row: K1, k2tog, k1, k3tog, k1, k2tog, k1 (7 sts).

Next row: Purl.
Next row: K1, k2tog, k1, k2tog, k1 (5 sts).
Next row: Purl.
Cast (bind) off.
Make another arm to match.

HEAD
Using yarn A doubled, cast on 9 sts.
Work 2 rows in st st.
Next row: Increase 1 st at each end of this and every following alt row until there are 21 sts.
Work a further 20 rows without shaping.
Next row: Decrease 1 st at each end of this and every following row until there are 9 sts.
Cast (bind) off.
Make another piece to match.

TAIL
Using yarn A doubled, follow pattern for Mousie Mousie's tail (see page 91).
Work until piece measures 35cm (13¾in).

HANDS AND FEET (2 pieces for each)
Using yarn B, cast on 20 sts and work in garter st for 20 rows.
Break yarn and draw through sts.
Fasten off.

FACE

Using yarn B, cast on 8 sts and work in st st.

K 1 row.

Next row: K1, p to last st, k1.

Next row: Increase 1 st at each end of this and every following row until there are 20 sts, then on following 4th row to make 22 sts.

Work 9 rows without further shaping.

Decrease 1 st at each end of next and 2 following alt rows (16 sts).

Work 1 row.

Next row: K8, turn work, k1, p to the last st, k1.

Working on these stitches only, decrease 1 st at each end of next and every following alt row (4 sts).

Next row: K1, p to last st, k1.

Next row: K.

Next row: P.

K2tog twice (2 sts).

Break yarn and draw through. Fasten off. Rejoin yarn to rem 8 sts and complete to match first side.

EARS

Using yarn A single, cast on 10 sts and work in garter st.

K 4 rows.

Next row: K2tog, k6, k2tog (8 sts).

Work 3 rows without shaping.

Next row: K2tog, k4, k2tog (6 sts).

Next row: K2tog, k2, k2tog (4 sts).

Next row: K2tog twice (2 sts). Break yarn and draw through. Fasten off. Make another ear to match.

WAISTCOAT

Using yarn C, cast on 30 sts and work in garter st.

K 1 row.

Next row: Increase 1 st at each end of row (32 sts).

Work 8 rows without shaping.

Shape armholes:

Next row: K7, cast (bind) off 2 sts, k10, cast (bind) off 2 sts, working on these 7 sts only.

Work 9 rows.

Next row: Cast (bind) off 1 st, work to end.

Work 1 row.

Next row: Cast (bind) off 1 st, work to end.

Work 3 rows.

Cast (bind) off.

Rejoin yarn to central 10 sts. Work 14 rows in garter st.

Cast (bind) off.

Rejoin yarn to rem 7 sts, reverse shaping to match first side.

SCARF

Using yarn D doubled, cast on 6 sts.
Work in garter st until scarf measures
approx. 25cm (10in).
Cast (bind) off.

TO MAKE UP MONKEY

Darn in all loose ends. Join centre
seams of body fronts and attach to back
with mattress stitch. Stuff firmly. Sew
head pieces together and graft on face.
Sew arm and leg seams using mattress
stitch and attach hands and feet. Using
the illustration as a guide, attach all
body pieces. Sew on tail. Sew shoulders
together on waistcoat and tie scarf
loosely around neck. Embroider facial
features.

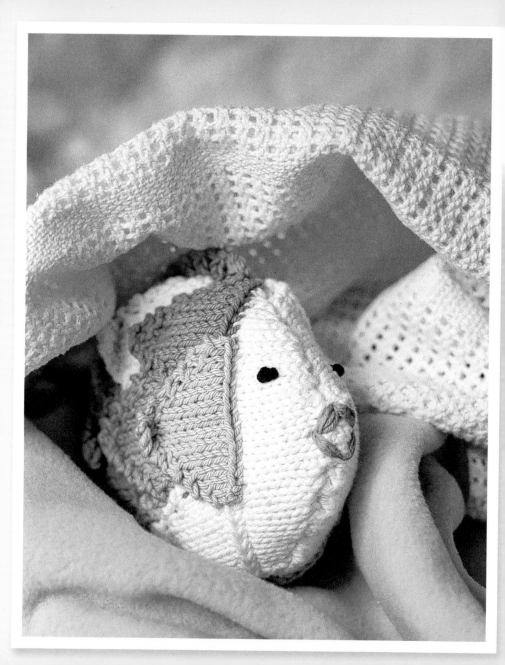

Robbie the Fish

Robbie's brightly coloured scales make him one of the best-looking fish in the sea. He is just the right size to tuck under your arm on a day out exploring dry land!

MATERIALS
50g balls of DK (light worsted) 100% cotton yarn: 2 x white (A), 1 x light blue (B), 1 x mid-blue (C), 1 x lilac (D) and 1 x gold (E)
Black embroidery thread for eyes
4mm (US: 6) needles
Toy stuffing

TENSION (GAUGE)
20 sts and 28 rows to 10cm (4in) measured over st st on 4mm (US: 6) needles.

MAIN BODY (make 2 pieces)
Using yarn A, cast on 8 sts and k 1 row. Beg with a p row, work in st st throughout.
Cast on 3 sts at beg of next 2 rows (14 sts).
Cast on 2 sts at beg of next 4 rows (22 sts).
Work 1 row.
Next row: Increase 1 st at each end of this and every following alt row until there are 26 sts.
Next row: P.
Next row: Increase 1 st at each end of this and following 4 alt rows until there are 30 sts.
Work a further 7 rows without shaping.
Next row: Decrease 1 st at each end of this and following 4th row (26 sts).
Work 1 row.
Next row: Decrease 1 st at each end of this and every following alt row until there are 22 sts.
Work 1 row.
Cast (bind) off 2 sts at beg of next 4 rows (14 sts).
Cast (bind) off 3 sts at beg of next 2 rows (8 sts).
Cast (bind) off rem 8 sts.

SCALES
24 scales are used on the fish (12 on each side), and they are knitted in yarns A, B, C and D.

Using the appropriate yarn, cast on 3 sts and k 2 rows.

Next row: Increase 1 st at each end of row (5 sts).

Next row: P.

Rep last 2 rows until there are 13 sts. Cast (bind) off.

FIN AND TAIL

The pieces are worked in the same way as the scales.

Using yarn E, cast on 8 sts and, working in k1, p1 rib, complete 1 row.

Next row: Increase 1 st at each end of this row (10 sts).

Cont increasing as before on every row until there are 20 sts.

Cast (bind) off.

TO MAKE UP THE FISH

Darn in all loose ends. Attach 12 of the fins to each side panel as illustrated. When joining the side panels, insert the fin along the top edge and the tail at the back. Stuff firmly. Use black embroidery thread for the eyes, and sew on lips made from a scrap of yarn E.

Mr Bumble

Mr Bumble is a jolly little bee. He is simple to knit and enjoys buzzing around the garden.

MATERIALS
50g balls of DK (light worsted) 100% cotton yarn: 1 x black (A) and 1 x gold (B)
White and pink embroidery thread for eyes and mouth
4mm (US: 6) needles
Toy stuffing

TENSION (GAUGE)
20 sts and 28 rows to 10cm (4in) measured over st st on 4mm (US: 6) needles.

BODY
TOP PANEL
Worked by alternating yarns A and B in 4 x 4-row st-st stripes.
Using yarn A, cast on 6 sts and work 2 rows in st st.
Increase in every st (12 sts).
Next row: P.
Increase in every st (24 sts).
Beg with a p row, work 29 rows in st st.
Decrease top:
Next row: K1, k2 tog, k8, k2tog, k8, k2tog, k1 (21 sts).
Beg with a p row, work 7 rows in st st.
Next row: K1, sl1, k1, psso, k15, k2tog, k1 (19 sts).
Next row: P.
Next row: K1, sl1, k1, psso, k13, k2tog, k1 (17 sts).
Next row: P.
Next row: K1, sl1, k1, psso, k11, k2tog, k1 (15 sts).
Next row: P.
Next row: K1, sl1,k1, psso, k9, k2tog, k1 (13 sts).
Next row: P.
Next row: Cast (bind) off 2 sts at beg of next 4 rows (5 sts).
Cast (bind) off remainder.

BOTTOM PANEL
Work as for top panel, using yarn A only.

HEAD (make 2 pieces)
Using yarn A, cast on 6 sts.
Work 2 rows in st st.
Next row: Increase 1 st at each end of

row (8 sts).

Work 10 rows in st st.

Next row: Decrease 1 st at each end of this row (6 sts).

Cast (bind) off.

LARGE WINGS

Using yarn A, cast on 12 sts.

K 2 rows.

Row 3: Increase 1 st at each end of row (14 sts).

Rep these 3 rows until there are 22 sts.

Next row: K2tog to end (11 sts).

Cast (bind) off.

Make another wing.

SMALL WINGS

Using yarn A, cast on 8 sts.

K 2 rows.

Row 3: Increase 1 st at each end of row (10 sts).

Rep these 3 rows until there are 18 sts.

Next row: K2tog to end (9 sts).

Cast (bind) off.

Make another wing.

TO MAKE UP THE BEE

Darn in all ends. Sew the body pieces together with mattress stitch, then stuff. Join the head sections and attach to the body. Use chain stitch to make antennae and knot the ends to form balls. Attach to head. Join the wings to the body. Embroider the eyes and mouth.

Teddy Bear

Create this enduring Teddy Bear to be someone's special friend. He will reward his owner with lots of love and loyalty. There are two different sweaters to make for him, so you can change his outfits and keep him looking stylish. He could also make a special gift for an adult bear fan.

Teddy

MATERIALS
50g balls of DK (light worsted) 100% wool in tweed effect: 4 x brown
Black embroidery thread for eyes and mouth
4mm (US: 6) needles
Toy stuffing

TENSION (GAUGE)
22 sts and 30 rows to 10cm (4in) measured over st st on 4mm (US: 6) needles.

HEAD
Cast on 6 sts.
Work in garter st throughout.
Work 1 row.
Next row: Increase in every st (12 sts).
Work 1 row.
Next row: K1, increase into each of the next 10 sts, k1 (22 sts).

Work 1 row.
Shape nose:
Next row: K1, inc 1, k7, inc 1, k6, inc 1, k7, inc 1, k1 (26 sts).
Next and every alt row: Work without shaping.
Next row: K1, inc 1, k9, inc 1, k6, inc 1, k9, inc 1, k1 (30 sts).
Next row: K1, inc 1, k11, inc 1, k6, inc 1, k11, inc 1, k1 (34 sts).
Next row: K1, inc 1, k13, inc 1, k6, inc 1, k13, inc 1, k1 (38 sts).
Next row: K1, inc 1, k15, inc 1, k6, inc 1, k15, inc 1, k1 (42 sts).
Work 2 rows without shaping.
Next row: (K1, k2tog) six times, k6, (k2tog, k1) six times (30 sts).
Shape head:
Next row: K11, inc 1, k1, inc 1, k6, inc 1, k1, inc 1, k11 (34 sts).
Next and every alt row: Work without shaping.
Next row: K12, inc 1, k1, inc 1, k8, inc 1,

k1, inc 1, k12 (38 sts).
Next row: K13, inc 1, k1, inc 1, k10, inc 1, k1, inc 1, k13 (42 sts).
Next row: K14, inc 1, k1, inc 1, k12, inc 1, k1, inc 1, k14 (46 sts).
Next row: K15, inc 1, k1, inc 1, k14, inc 1, k1, inc 1, k15 (50 sts).
Next row: K16, inc 1, k1, inc 1, k16, inc 1, k1, inc 1, k16 (54 sts).
Next row: K6 (inc 1, k1) thirteen times, k16, (k1, inc 1) thirteen times, k6 (80 sts).
Work a further 13 rows without shaping.
Shape back:
Next row: (K8, k2tog) to end (72 sts).
Next and every alt row: Work without shaping.
Next row: (K7, k2tog) to end (64 sts).
Next row: (K6, k2tog) to end (56 sts).
Next row: (K5, k2tog) to end (48 sts).
Next row: (K4, k2tog) to end (40 sts).
Next row: (K3, k2tog) to end (32 sts).
Next row: (K2, k2tog) to end (24 sts).
Next row: (K1, k2tog) to end (16 sts).
Next row: (K2tog) to end (8 sts).
Cast (bind) off.

BODY (make 2 pieces)
Cast on 9 sts.
Work 2 rows in garter st.
Next row: Increase 1 st at each end of row (11 sts).

Work 1 row.
Rep the last 2 rows four times (19 sts).
Next row: K9, increase before and after centre st, k9 (21 sts).
Cont to increase in this manner (either side of centre st) on every alt row until there are 45 sts.
Work a further 31 rows without shaping.
Next row: Decrease 1 st at each end of this and every following alt row until there are 21 sts.
Next row: (K2tog) five times, k1, (k2tog) five times.
Cast (bind) off.

ARMS (make 2)
Cast on 7 sts.
Work 1 row.
Next row: K1 (inc 1, k1) to end (13 sts).
Rep last 2 rows once more (25 sts).
Work 1 row.
Next row: K6, inc 1, k1, inc 1, k11, inc 1, k1, inc 1, k6 (29 sts).
Work a further 28 rows without shaping.
Shape top of arms:
Decrease 1 st at each end of this and every following 6th row until there are 17 sts, then on every following 3rd row until there are 11 sts.
Next row: K1 (k2tog) to end (6 sts).
Cast (bind) off.

LEGS (make 2)

Cast on 46 sts.

Work 12 rows.

Next row: Decrease 1 st at each end of row (44 sts).

Cast (bind) off 2 sts at beg of next 2 rows (40 sts).

Cast (bind) off 4 sts at beg of next 2 rows (32 sts).

Work a further 31 rows without shaping.

Cast (bind) off 4 sts at beg of next 2 rows (24 sts).

Cast (bind) off 4 sts at beg of next 2 rows (16 sts).

Cast (bind) off rem sts.

PAW PADS (make 2)

Cast on 5 sts.

Work in garter st.

Work 1 row.

Next row: Increase 1 st at each end of this and every following alt row until there are 13 sts.

Work a further 6 rows without shaping.

Next row: Decrease 1 st at each end of every alt row until there are 8 sts.

Cast (bind) off.

EARS (make 4 pieces, 2 for each ear)

Beg at top of ear, cast on 16 sts.

Work in garter st.

Work 1 row.

Next row: Increase 1 st at each end of row (18 sts).

Work 1 row.

Rep last 2 rows until there are 24 sts.

Work a further 2 rows without shaping.

Next row: Decrease 1 st at each end of this and every following alt row, until there are 16 sts.

Cast (bind) off.

TO MAKE UP THE BEAR

Darn in all loose ends. Join the head seam and stuff firmly. Sew the ear sections together and position on the head as illustrated. Leaving the neck open, join all body pieces and attach the head. Join both leg seams, inserting the pads at the base, and stuff firmly. Repeat with the arms. Attach the arms and legs to body, ensuring that Teddy will sit steadily. Embroider on the eyes and nose.

Pink sweater

MATERIALS

50g balls of DK (light worsted) 100% wool in tweed effect: 2 x pink (A)
50g balls of DK (light worsted) 100% wool: 1 x white (B)
4mm (US: 6) needles
2 small buttons

TENSION (GAUGE)

22 sts and 30 rows to 10cm (4in) measured over st st on 4mm (US: 6) needles.

BACK

Using yarn A, cast on 50 sts.
Work 8 rows in k2, p2 rib.
Cont in st st and work 40 rows.

Shoulder shaping:
Cast (bind) off 15 sts at beg of next 2 rows (20 sts).
Cast (bind) off rem sts.

FRONT

Using yarn A, cast on 50 sts.
Work 8 rows in k2, p2 rib.
Cont in st st, and work 4 rows.
Using Fair Isle technique and contrast yarn where indicated, work the next 11 rows from the chart.
Cont in st st until 34 rows have been completed from top of rib.
Divide for neck:
K20, cast (bind) off central 10 sts, k to end.
Using these 20 sts only, work 1 row.
Next row: Decrease 1 st at neck edge on

Pink sweater motif

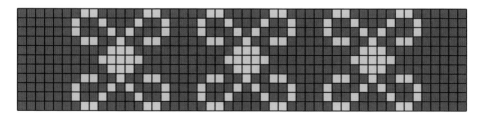

■ A   □ B

this and following two alt rows (17 sts).
Work 3 rows in st st.
Cast (bind) off.
Rejoin yarn to rem 20 sts and work to match first side, reversing shaping.

SLEEVES (make 2)
Using yarn A, cast on 40 sts.
Work 6 rows in k2, p2 rib.
Cont in st st, and work 20 rows.
Cast (bind) off.

NECKBAND
Join right-hand shoulder using mattress stitch.
With RS facing, pick up 54 sts evenly around the neck.
Work 5 rows in k2, p2 rib.
Cast (bind) off in pattern.

SHOULDER
Catch left side shoulder together at sleeve edge (approx 2.5cm/1in).
Pick up 32 sts evenly from neck edge, down to sleeve edge and back up to other side of neckband, and knit.
Next row: P.
Next row (buttonhole row): K23, yfwd, k2tog, k3, yfwd, k2tog, k2.
Next row: P.
Cast (bind) off.

TO MAKE UP SWEATER
Darn in all ends and sew buttons to shoulder. Fold sleeves in half lengthways and, starting at the centre of the shoulder, sew on using mattress stitch. Join the side and sleeve seams.

Blue sweater

MATERIALS
50g balls of DK (light worsted) 100% wool in tweed effect: 2 x blue
4mm (US: 6) needles
Cable needle

Tension (gauge)
22 sts and 30 rows to 10cm (4in) measured over st st on 4mm (US: 6) needles.

BACK
Cast on 50 sts.
Work 8 rows in k2, p2 rib.
Cont in st st and work 42 rows.
Work 6 rows in k2, p2 rib.
Cast (bind) off.

FRONT
Cast on 50 sts.
Work 8 rows in k2, p2 rib.

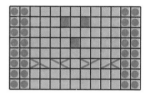

Blue sweater motif

□ K on RS, p on WS

◉ P on RS, k on WS

▪ Make bobble (k1, p1, k1, p1, k1) in stitch to make 5 sts from one. Turn, p5, turn, and pass 2nd, 3rd, 4th and 5th sts over 1st st one at a time, then knit into the back of it.

⟩⟩⟩⟩ Sl next 2 sts on to cable needle and hold at front. K2, then p2 from cable needle.

⟩⟩⟩⟩ Sl next 2 sts on to cable needle and hold at back. P2, then k2 from cable needle.

Cont in st st and work 42 rows, inserting cable panel in centre of front panel – work 19 sts; set panel 13 sts; work 18 sts (50 sts).
Work 6 rows in k2, p2 rib.
Cast (bind) off.

SLEEVES
Work as for pink sweater.

TO MAKE UP SWEATER
Darn in all loose ends. Join front and back panels by a 2.5cm (1in) seam at shoulders, using mattress stitch to form slash neck. Attach sleeves.

Ricky the Rabbit

This delightful, floppy-eared bunny likes to dress to impress his friends in the warren, loves meeting new people, and has a great sense of humour. Who are you going to introduce him to?

MATERIALS

50g balls of DK (light worsted) cotton and acrylic blend: 2 x cream (A) and 2 x fawn (B)
Black embroidery thread for eyes and mouth
50cm (19¾in) length of broad double satin ribbon
4.5mm (US: 7) needles
Toy stuffing

TENSION (GAUGE)

18 sts and 25 rows to 10cm (4in) measured over st st on 4.5mm (US: 7) needles.

Rabbit

BODY – FRONT

Using yarn A, cast on 20 sts and work 2 rows in st st.
Increase 1 st at each end of next and following alt row (24 sts).

Cont without further shaping until work measures 15cm (6in) from beginning.
Next row: Decrease 1 st at each end of next and every following 4th row until there are 12 sts.
Work 3 rows in st st.
Cast (bind) off.

BODY – BACK

Using yarn B, cast on 24 sts and work 2 rows in st st.
Increase 1 st at each end of this and following alt row (28 sts).
Cont without further shaping until work measures 15cm (6in) from beginning.
Next row: Decrease 1 st at each end of next and every following 4th row until there are 16 sts.
Work 3 rows in st st.
Cast (bind) off.

HEAD – BACK

Using yarn B, cast on 12 sts and work 2 rows in st st.

Next row: Increase 1 st at each end of row (14 sts).
Rep this increase on every other row until there are 20 sts.
Work a further 8 rows in st st without shaping.
Next row: Decrease 1 st at each end of this and every following alt row until there are 6 sts.
Cast (bind) off.

HEAD – FRONT

Using yarn B, cast on 6 sts and work 2 rows in st st.
Next row: K1, increase 1 st, k to end of row (7 sts).
Next row: K1, p to last st, increase 1 st, k1 (8 sts).
Rep the last 2 rows four times (16 sts).
Work a further 2 rows without shaping.
Next row: K2tog, k to end (15 sts).
Next row: P.
Rep the last 2 rows four times (9 sts).
Cont to decrease on the same edge until 3 sts remain.
Next row: K1, p2tog.
Cast (bind) off.
Work another piece the same, reversing all shaping.

EARS

Each made in two sections (one in yarn A and one in yarn B).
Using the appropriate yarn, cast on 5 sts and k one row.
Next row: K1, p to last st, k1.
Cont working in st st, increasing 1 st at each end of next and every following 4th row, until there are 11 sts.
Work a further 11 rows without shaping.
Next row: Decrease at each end of this and every following 8th row until 3 sts remain.
Next row: K1, p2tog, psso. Fasten off.

FEET (make 2)

Using yarn B, cast on 8 sts and work 2 rows in st st.
Next row: Increase 1 st at each end of row (10 sts).
Cont working in st st for a further 31 rows without shaping.
Cast (bind) off.

ARMS (make 2)

Using yarn B, follow arm pattern for Mousie Mousie (page 90).

TAIL

Make a pompom using yarn A. Cut 2 circles of cardboard, approx. 20cm (8in)

in diameter, and cut out a circle in the centre of each to make a ring. Hold both rings together and start wrapping yarn around the ring, threading it through the centre, until completely covered. Position the point of a pair of scissors in the yarn loops so that you can cut through them, going in between the cardboard rings. Separate the rings slightly and tie yarn tightly inside the cut sections. Remove cardboard and fluff up the pompom. Sew to back of rabbit.

TO MAKE UP THE RABBIT

Join body pieces together using mattress stitch, then stuff. Join the side seams of both feet and arms, and pad slightly. Attach the arms to the shoulders of the rabbit and sew on the feet as illustrated. To form the head, sew the shaped sides of the two front pieces together, then sew the straight edge to the back piece, leaving the cast-on edges open to stuff. Attach to body. Sew a yarn A and yarn B ear piece together. Repeat to make the other ear and attach to head. Embroider the features. Tie the ribbon around the neck.

Sleeveless top

MATERIALS

50g ball of DK (light worsted) cotton and acrylic blend: 1 x light blue
4.5mm (US: 7) needles

Tension (gauge)

18 sts and 25 rows to 10cm measured over stocking stitch on 4.5mm (US: 7) needles.

BACK

Cast on 22 sts.

Knit 2 rows.

Next row: Cont in st st until work measures 8cm (3in) ending with a WS row *.

Shape top of back:
K1, k2tog, work to last 3 sts, k2tog, k1 (20 sts).
Work 3 rows in st st.
Rep the last 4 rows once more (18 sts).
Work the decrease row once more (16 sts).

Next row: P.
Cast (bind) off.

FRONT

Work as for Back until you reach *.
Shape top and divide for neck: K1, k2tog, k5, k2tog, k1.
Turn work and work on these 9 sts only.
Work 3 rows in st st.
Next row: K1, k2tog, k3, k2tog, k1 (7 sts).
Work 3 rows in st st.
Next row: K1, k2tog, k1, k2tog, k1 (5 sts).
Work 3 rows in st st.
Cast (bind) off.
Rejoin yarn to rem sts, complete to match first side and cast (bind) off.

TO MAKE UP RABBIT'S TOP

Darn in all ends. Join shoulder seams using mattress stitch. Join side seams.

Polly the Penguin

Polly the Penguin is just the right size for little hands. She's ready to waddle into a new home and become a cherished companion. She has lots of stories to tell about her life in the Arctic, exploring snowy wastes and diving through the ice.

MATERIALS

50g balls of DK (light worsted) 100% cotton yarn: 1 x black (A), 1 x white (B) and 1 x gold (C)
Black embroidery thread
4mm (US: 6) needles
Toy stuffing

TENSION (GAUGE)

20 sts and 28 rows to 10cm (4in) measured over st st on 4mm (US: 6) needles.

BACK

Using yarn A, cast on 20 sts.
Working in st st, complete 26 rows.
Decrease 1 st at each end of next and every following 6th row until there are 10 sts.
Work 1 row *.
Decrease 1 st at each end of next and every following alt row until there are 6 sts.

Work 1 row.
Next row: K2tog, k2, k2tog (4 sts).
Next row: P.
Cast (bind) off.

FRONT

Using yarn B, work as Back until *.
Cast (bind) off.

BEAK TOP

Using yarn C, cast on 18 sts.
Work 4 rows in st st.
Decrease 1 st at each end of next 4 rows (10 sts).
Work 12 rows without further shaping.
Decrease 1 st at each end of next 3 rows (4 sts).
Next row: P.
Cast (bind) off.

BEAK BOTTOM

Using yarn C, cast on 5 sts.
Work 4 rows in st st.

Next row: K2tog, k1, k2tog (3 sts).
Starting with a p row, work 13 rows in
st st.
Next row: K1, k2tog (2 sts).
Next row: Purl.
Break yarn off, draw through loops and
fasten off.

FEET (make 2 in yarn A and 2 in yarn C)

Using the appropriate yarn, cast on 7 sts.
Work 2 rows in st st.
Increase 1 st at each end of this and
every following alt row until there are
11 sts.
Work 5 rows in st st.
Decrease 1 st at each end of next and
every following alt row until there are
5 sts.
Purl.
Cast (bind) off.

LEFT FLIPPER

Using yarn A, cast on 3 sts.
Work 1 row in purl.
Next row: * Increase 1 st at beg of this
and every following alt row until there
are 10 sts.
Work 16 rows in st st.
Shape top of flipper:
Work to last 3 sts, k2tog, k1 (9 sts).

Next row: P.
Cont to decrease at the end of next and
every following alt row until there are
5 sts.
Work 1 row.
Cast (bind) off.

RIGHT FLIPPER

Work as Left Flipper to *.
Increase 1 st at end of this and every
following alt row until there are 10 sts.
Work 16 rows in st st.
Complete to match left side, reversing
shaping at the top.

TO MAKE UP PENGUIN

Darn in all loose ends. Join main body
panels using mattress stitch, leaving the
top open. Stuff firmly. Join beak parts,
stuffing them slightly. Attach the beak
to the top of the body as illustrated,
and stitch the eyes in black embroidery
thread. Using mattress stitch, join the
yarn A and C feet pieces, padding them
firmly. Close them completely and then
attach to the main body, with yarn C
showing on top. Apply flippers to each
side of the main body along side seam.

Kangaroo and Baby Roo

This cute and cuddly double act have travelled a long way from sunny Australia. Kangaroo has prepared for chilly breezes with a dashing scarf; Baby Roo just snuggles down in her pouch. They're looking for someone to show them all the sights in their new home country.

MATERIALS

50g balls of DK (light worsted) cotton and acrylic blend: 4 x gold (A) and 1 x cream (B)
50g ball of 4ply (sport-weight) 100% wool in tweed effect: 1 x green (C)
Black embroidery thread for eyes
3mm (US: 3), 3.75mm (US: 5) and 4mm (US: 6) needles
Toy stuffing

TENSION (GAUGE)

For kangaroo: 20 sts and 28 rows to 10cm (4in) using yarn A measured over st st on 4mm (US: 6) needles.

For scarf: 28 sts and 40 rows to 10cm (4in) using yarn C measured over st st on 3mm (US: 2) needles .

Kangaroo

BODY – SIDE

Using yarn A and 4mm (US: 6) needles, cast on 34 sts.
Work 9 rows in st st.
Next row: Cast (bind) off 16 sts, p to end (18 sts).
Row 11: K to last st, inc at end of row (19 sts).
Row 12: Inc 1 st at beg of row, p to end (20 sts).
Row 13: K to last st, inc at end of row (21 sts).
Row 14: As row 12 (22 sts).
Row 15: K.
Row 16: As row 12 (23 sts).
Row 17: K.
Row 18: P (24 sts).
Work a further 15 rows in st st without shaping.
Row 34: P2tog, work to end (23 sts).
Row 35: K.

Row 36: Cast (bind) off 7 sts, p to end (16 sts).
Row 37: K to last st, inc at end of row (17 sts).
Row 38: P.
Row 39: As row 37 (18 sts).
Work a further 3 rows in st st without shaping.
Row 43: K2tog, k to end (17 sts).
Row 44: P.
Row 45: As row 43 (16 sts).
Row 46: P.
Row 47: As row 43 (15 sts).
Row 48: P.
Row 49: As row 43 (14 sts).
Work a further 8 rows in st st without shaping.
Row 58: Dec 1 st at beg of row, work to end (13 sts).
Row 59: Dec 1 st at beg of row, work to end (12 sts).
Work a further 6 rows in st st without shaping.
Row 66: Cast on 7 sts, work to end (19 sts).
Row 67: K.
Row 68: P2tog, work to end (18 sts).
Row 69: K.
Row 70: As row 68 (17 sts).
Row 71: K.
Row 72: As row 68 (16 sts).
Row 73: K2tog, work to end.

Row 74: As row 68 (15 sts).
Row 75: K2tog, work to end (14 sts).
Row 76: K2tog, work to last 2 sts, k2tog (12 sts).
Row 77: K2tog at each end of row (10 sts).
Cast (bind) off.
Make another piece, reversing all shaping.

BODY – FRONT

Using yarn B and 4mm (US: 6) needles, cast on 40 sts.
Work 9 rows in st st.
Row 10: Cast (bind) off 16 sts, work to end (24 sts).
Row 11: Cast (bind) off 16 sts, work to end (8 sts).
Row 12: Increase 1 st at each end of row (10 sts).
Row 13: Increase 1 st at each end of row (12 sts).
Row 14: Increase 1 st at each end of row (14 sts).
Row 15: K.
Row 16: Increase 1 st at each end of row (16 sts).
Row 17: K.
Row 18: Increase 1 st at each end of row (18 sts).
Row 19: K.

Row 20: Increase 1 st at each end of row (20 sts).

Work a further 17 rows without shaping.

Row 38: Cast (bind) off 6 sts at beg of row, work to end (14 sts).

Row 39: Cast (bind) off 6 sts at beg of row, work to end (8 sts).

Work on these 8 sts until work measures the same as the body sides to beg of head shaping.

Cast (bind) off.

BODY – BASE

Using yarn A and 4mm (US: 6) needles, cast on 10 sts.

Work 18 rows in st st.

Cast (bind) off.

EARS (make 2)

Using yarn A and 4mm (US: 6) needles, cast on 7 sts.

Work 8 rows in garter st.

Next row: K2tog, k3, k2tog (5 sts).

Next row: K.

Next row: K2tog, k1, k2tog (3 sts).

Next row: K.

Next row: K2tog, k1 (2 sts).

Next row: K2tog (1 st).

Fasten off.

ARMS (make 2)

Using yarn A and 4mm (US: 6) needles, follow arm instructions for Mousie Mousie (page 90).

TAIL

Using yarn A and 4mm (US: 6) needles, follow tail instructions for Mousie Mousie (page 91) and work 28 rows without shaping.

POUCH

Using yarn A and 4mm (US: 6) needles, cast on 14 sts.

Work in moss st (seed st) for 1 row.

Next row: Cont in moss st (seed st) and increase 1 st at each end of row (16 sts).

Work 2 rows without shaping.

Cont to increase 1 st at each end of next and every following 3rd row until there are 22 sts.

Next row: Work in k1, p1 rib to end.

Work 2 rows in rib without further shaping.

Cast (bind) off in pattern.

SCARF

Using yarn C and 3mm (US: 2) needles, cast on 7 sts and work in garter st for approx 20cm (8in).

Cast (bind) off.

TO MAKE UP KANGAROO

Darn in all loose ends. Sew the two body sides together using mattress stitch, and attach to the front panel. Stuff firmly, ensuring the base is squarely placed at the bottom. Attach the pouch to the body using mattress stitch. Join the arm and tail seams and stuff. Sew arms to main body at shoulder, and position tail at base. Embroider eyes. Tie scarf loosely around neck.

Baby Roo

BODY – SIDE PANEL

Starting at feet, using yarn A and 3.75mm (US: 5) needles, cast on 10 sts.

Work 4 rows in st st.
Row 5: Cast (bind) off 5 sts, k to end
(5 sts).
Work a further 7 rows without shaping.
Row 13: Cast on 4 sts, k to end (9 sts).
Work a further 3 rows without shaping.
Row 17: Cast (bind) off 4 sts, k to end
(5 sts).
Work a further 2 rows without shaping.
Row 20: P2tog, p3 (4 sts).
Row 21: K.
Row 22: P2tog, p2 (3 sts).
Row 23: Cast on 4 sts, k to end (7 sts).
Row 24: P2tog, p to end (6 sts).
Row 25: K2tog, k to end (5 sts).
Row 26: P.
Row 27: K2tog, k3.
Cast (bind) off.
Work second side to match this,
reversing all shaping.

BODY – FRONT PANEL
Using yarn A and 3.75mm (US: 5)
needles, cast on 14 sts.
Work 4 rows in st st.
Row 5: Cast (bind) off 5 sts, k to end (9 sts).
Row 6: Cast (bind) off 5 sts, p to end (4 sts).
Work a further 8 rows without shaping.
Row 15: Cast on 4 sts, k to end (8 sts).
Row 16: Cast on 4 sts, p to end (12 sts).
Work a further 3 rows without shaping.

Row 20: Cast (bind) off 4 sts, p to end
(8 sts).
Row 21: Cast (bind) off 4 sts, k to end
(4 sts).
Row 22: P2tog twice.
Row 23: K2tog, fasten off.

EARS (make 2)
Using yarn A and 3.75mm (US: 5)
needles, cast on 2 sts.
Work 4 rows in garter st.
Next row: K2tog twice.
Next row: K2.
Next row: K2tog, fasten off.

TAIL
Using yarn A and 3.75mm (US: 5)
needles, cast on 4 sts.
Work 16 rows in garter st.
Next row: K2tog twice.
Next row: K2.
Next row: K2tog, fasten off.

TO MAKE UP BABY ROO
Darn in all loose ends. Sew the two sides
together along back seam and leave a
small opening for stuffing. Sew in the
front panel, starting at bottom feet. Stuff
firmly and close the seam in the back. Sew
on the ears, folding them slightly at the
base. Attach the tail. Embroider the eyes.

Loulou the Elephant

Share all your secrets with Loulou, a gentle woolly giant, who will never forget them. This sturdy creature is a delight to knit.

MATERIALS

50g balls of DK (light worsted) 100% wool in tweed effect: 4 x grey (A)
Small amount of 4ply (sport-weight) 100% cotton in white (B)
3mm (US: 2) and 4mm (US: 6) needles
Toy stuffing

TENSION (GAUGE)

22 sts and 30 rows to 10cm (4in) using yarn A measured over st st on 4mm (US: 6) needles.

NOTE

Use yarn A and 4mm (US: 6) needles for all parts of elephant except for the tusks.

HEAD – SIDE SECTIONS (make 2)

Cast on 25 sts.
Knit 1 row.
Cont in st st throughout. Increase 1 st at each end of the next 2 rows (29 sts).
Work a further 11 rows without shaping.
Next row: Increase 1 st at each end of row (31 sts).

Work a further 12 rows without shaping.
Next row: K2tog at each end of row (29 sts).
Work a further 14 rows without shaping.
Next row: K2tog at each end of the following 5 rows (19 sts).
Cast (bind) off.

HEAD – CENTRE GUSSET, TOP

Cast on 7 sts.
Work 7 rows in st st.
Next row: Increase 1 st at each end of row (9 sts).
Rep last 8 rows seven times (23 sts).
Work a further 30 rows without shaping.
Next row: Decrease 1 st at each end of row (21 sts).
Work a further 11 rows without shaping.
Rep the decrease row eight times (5 sts).
Cast (bind) off.

HEAD – CENTRE GUSSET, UNDER TRUNK

Cast on 7 sts.
Work 11 rows in st st.

Next row: Increase 1 st at each end of row.
Rep the last 12 rows five times.
Cast (bind) off.

EARS (make 2)

Ears are worked in garter st throughout.
Cast on 17 sts.
Knit 1 row.
Next row: Increase 1 st at each end of the following 6 rows (29 sts).
Next row: K to last st, increase twice (31 sts).
Work a further 18 rows without shaping.
Next row: (K2tog, k3) to last st, k1 (25 sts).
Next row: K2tog three times, k5, k2tog three times.
Cast (bind) off rem sts.

BODY – FRONT AND BACK

Cast on 20 sts.
Work in st st throughout.
Work 2 rows.
Next row: Increase 1 st at each end of this and every following alt row until there are 30 sts.
Next row: Increase 1 st at each end of this and every following 4th row until

there are 40 sts.
Work a further 24 rows without shaping.
Next row: Decrease 1 st at each end of this and every following 4th row until there are 20 sts.
Next row: K2tog, k to end.
Cast (bind) off.

ARMS (make 2)

Cast on 25 sts.
Work 22 rows in st st.
Cast (bind) off.

LEGS (make 2)
Cast on 30 sts.
Work 30 rows in st st.
Cast (bind) off.

PADS – FOR ARMS (make 2)
Cast on 6 sts.
Work 2 rows in st st.
Next row: Increase 1 st at each end of row (8 sts).
Next row: P.
Next row: Increase 1 st at each end of row (10 sts).
Work a further 5 rows without shaping.
Next row: Decrease 1 st at each end of following 2 alt rows (6 sts).
Cast (bind) off.

PADS – FOR LEGS (make 2)
Cast on 6 sts.
Work 2 rows in st st.
Next row: Increase 1 st at each end of this and following 2 alt rows (12 sts).
Work a further 5 rows without shaping.
Next row: Decrease 1 st at each end of this and following 2 alt rows (6 sts).
Cast (bind) off.

TAIL
Cast on 7 sts.
Work 14 rows in st st.

Next row: Decrease 1 st at each end of this and every following 4th row until there are 3 sts.
Work a further 3 rows without shaping.
Break yarn and draw through rem sts.
Fasten off. Cut short lengths of yarn, knot together, place in the point of the tail, and sew side seam using mattress stitch.

TUSKS (make 2)
Using yarn B and 3mm (US: 2) needles, cast on 7 sts.
Work in st st for 30 rows.
Next row: K1, k2tog, k1, k2tog, k1 (5 sts).
Next row: P.
Next row: K2tog, k1, k2tog (3 sts).
Next row: P.
Next row: K3tog and fasten off.

TO MAKE UP THE ELEPHANT
Darn in all loose ends. Join all pieces using mattress stitch. Attach sides of head to main gusset. Insert lower gusset and stuff, leaving neck edges open. Join the body sections and sew on the head. Sew the side seams of arms and legs and insert pads; stuff. Attach to body (make sure elephant will sit on a flat surface). Sew on tail. Join tusk seams and draw up to make the tusk curve slightly. Sew on under the trunk. Add features.

Mousie Mousie

Childhood memories have been recaptured in this cheeky little mouse – my brothers kept mice and had lots of fun with them! Mousie Mousie is a personable character who sports a woolly scarf to keep him snug. He has a friendly face, a slithery tail and is good company for any child.

MATERIALS

50g balls of DK (light worsted) 100% cotton: 1 x fawn (A) and 1 x cream (B)
50g ball of DK (light worsted) 100% wool in tweed effect: 1 x green (C)
Oddments of black embroidery thread for eyes
4mm (US: 6) needles
2 x 4mm (US: 6) double-pointed needles

TENSION (GAUGE)

20 sts and 28 rows to 10cm (4in) in yarn A measured over st st on 4mm (US: 6) needles.

HEAD (make 2 pieces)

Note: this piece is knitted in reverse st st.
Using yarn A, cast on 17 sts.
Work 2 rows in st st.
Inc 1 st at each end of next and every following alt row until there are 27 sts.
Work 4 rows without shaping.
Next row: K1, (k2tog) twice, k to last 3 sts, k2tog, k1 (24 sts).
Next row: P.
Rep last 2 rows once more (21 sts).
Decrease 1 st at each end of next and every following alt row until there are 13 sts.
Next row: P.
Cast (bind) off 4 sts at beg of next 2 rows (5 sts).
Cast (bind) off rem 5 sts.

EARS (make 2)

Using yarn A, cast on 7 sts.
Work 2 rows in garter st.
Increase in first and last st of next row (9 sts).
Next row: K.
Increase in first and last st of next row (11 sts).
Next row: K.
Work 3 increase rows as before (17 sts).
Work 3 rows in garter st.
K2tog at each end of every row until

there are 9 sts.
Work 1 row in garter st.
Cast (bind) off.

BODY – FRONT

Using yarn B, cast on 5 sts. Work in st st.
Increase either side of centre stitch (7 sts).
Work 1 row.
Increase at beg and end of row, and as
before on either side of centre st (11 sts).
Work 1 row.
Rep last 2 rows until there are 39 sts.
Work 2 rows without shaping.
Decrease 1 st at each end of work on next
and every alt row until there are 29 sts.
Decrease on either side of centre st only,
on next and every alt row until 17 sts
remain.
Work 1 row.
Cast (bind) off.

BODY – BACK

Using yarn A, cast on 5 sts.
Row 1: Increase in every st.
Row 2: P.
Row 3: Increase 1 st at each end of next
and every alt row until there are 22 sts.
Work 4 rows in st st.
Dec 1 st at each end of row (20 sts).
Work 1 row.
Rep last 2 rows until there are 14 sts.

Cont without shaping until work
matches front body section.
Cast (bind) off.

ARMS (make 2)

Using yarn A, cast on 6 sts.
Work 2 rows in st st.
Increase 1 st at each end of next and
following alt rows until there are 14 sts.
Work 1 row.
Work 16 rows in st st.
K1 (k2tog) six times, k1 (8 sts).
Work 1 row without shaping.
K2tog to end (4 sts).
Break thread and draw through rem sts
and secure.

FEET (make 2)

Using yarn A, cast on 8 sts.
Work 2 rows in st st.
Increase in first and last st of next row
(10 sts).
Work 18 rows in st st.
Cast (bind) off.

SCARF

Using yarn C, cast on 10 sts.
Work in garter st to length required:
approx. 30cm (12in).
Cast (bind) off.

TAIL

Using two double-pointed needles and yarn B, cast on 7 sts.

Knit to end. Instead of turning work, slide from one end of the needle to the other, keeping right side facing at all times, and continue to knit. This forms a tube.

Knit to desired length. Cast (bind) off.

TO MAKE UP MOUSIE

MOUSIE

Join head pieces using mattress stitch and stuff. Join the front and back body pieces in the same manner and secure to head. Sew on the ears and tail. Join the arm seams and stuff the arms slightly; then sew into position. Join the seams of the feet and sew the pieces into a round. Sew to body, ensuring that they are in a position for the mouse to stand. Darn in the ends of the scarf and wrap around. Sew eyes and nose, using black embroidery thread as illustrated.

Reggie the Snake

Have fun with this easy-to-knit snake. He will bring a smile to the face of any nature-loving child.

MATERIALS

50g balls of DK (light worsted) 100% wool in tweed effect: 2 x green (A) and 1 x red (B)
Oddments of yarn or embroidery thread for eyes and detail on back
4mm (US: 6) needles
Toy stuffing

TENSION (GAUGE)

20 sts and 28 rows to 10cm (4in) measured over st st on 4mm (US: 6) needles.

MAIN BODY

Using yarn A, cast on 7 sts.
Work 2 rows in st st.
Row 3: Increase 1 st at each end of work (9 sts).
Row 4: P.
Row 5: K.
Row 6: P.
Row 7: Increase 1 st at each end of work (11 sts).
Rep last 4 rows once more until there are 13 sts.
Cont in st st for a further 13 rows without shaping.
Next row: Increase 1 st at each end of row (15 sts).
Work a further 13 rows without shaping.
Increase on next and every 14th row until there are 29 sts.
Work without further shaping until snake measures 104cm (41in) from cast-on, ending on a purl row.
Shape head:
With RS facing, k14, cast (bind) off 1 st and k to end.
Working on the first 14 sts only, p.
Next row: K2tog, work to last 2 sts, k2tog (12 sts).
Work 3 rows without shaping.
Rep last 4 rows until 4 sts remain.
Cast (bind) off.
Rejoin yarn to rem 14 sts and complete to match first side.

MOUTH LINING

Using yarn B, cast on 4 sts.

Work 2 rows in st st.
Next row: Increase 1 st at each end of row (6 sts).
Work 3 rows in st st.
Next row: Increase 1 st at each end of row (8 sts).
Rep last 4 rows until there are 28 sts.
Work a further 12 rows without shaping.
With RS facing, decrease 1 st at each end of row.

Work 3 rows in st st.
Rep last 4 rows until 4 sts remain.
Cast (bind) off.

TO MAKE UP SNAKE

Darn in all loose ends. Join side seams using mattress stitch and stuff firmly. Insert mouth piece and slightly pad head. Darn eyes and embroider detail on the back of the snake as illustrated.

Nursery Toys

Each of these projects is designed for a baby or young child. From the starfish to the finger puppets, they're all wonderfully easy to knit. They can be given a character of their own by trying out different colours and facial expressions. The nursery balls and blocks are classic toys that any parent would be delighted to have for their new baby.

Starfish

When I lived by the beach, I always hoped to find a beautiful starfish just like this one among the pebbles. Keep him to remind you of sunny days by the sea. He is ideal for a baby or a young child to cuddle, and could even make a great doorstop!

MATERIALS
50g balls of DK (light worsted) cotton and acrylic blend: 1 x cream, 1 x light blue and 1 x sea blue
4.5mm (US: 7) needles
Toy stuffing

TENSION (GAUGE)
18 sts and 25 rows to 10cm (4in) measured over st st on 4.5mm (US: 7) needles.

NOTE
Knit ten panels: five are cream; five are a mixture of blues.

PANEL
Cast on 3 sts and work 2 rows in st st.

Next row: Increase 1 st at each end of next and every following 6th row until there are 19 sts.
Next row: P.
Shape top of panel:
K1, k2tog, k to last 3 sts, k2tog, k1 (17 sts).
Next row: P.
Rep last 2 rows until 5 sts remain.
K1, k2tog, pass stitch back from the right-hand needle to the left-hand needle, k2tog, k1 (3 sts).
Break yarn and draw through.

TO MAKE UP THE STARFISH
Darn in all ends. Join all sections, leaving adequate seams to allow for stuffing. Close all seams using mattress stitch.

Nursery Ball

These appealing knitted toys will be a welcome addition to any nursery. They are made in a combination of hearts and stripes.

MATERIALS
Ball with hearts:
50g balls of 4ply (sport-weight) 100% cotton: 1 x white (A) and 1 x sea green (B)

Ball with stripes:
50g balls of 4ply (sport-weight) 100% cotton: 1 x white, 1 x muted pink and 1 x sky blue

3mm (US: 2) needles
Toy stuffing

TENSION (GAUGE)
23 sts and 32 rows to 10cm (4in) measured over st st on 3mm (US: 2) needles.

NOTE
Each ball is made up of 6 panels and requires approx. 50g of yarn.

PANEL
Cast on 1 st, k1.
Next row: Purl into front, back and front (3 sts).

Cont in st st, increasing 1 st at each end of next and following 2 alt rows (9 sts). Work 2 rows without shaping. Increase 1 st at each end of next and following 3rd row, then at each end of following 4th row (15 sts). Work 5 rows without further shaping. Increase at each end of next and following 6th row (19 sts). Work 9 rows without further shaping. (Set heart motif within these 9 straight rows if required – follow chart.) Decrease once at each end of next and every following 6th row until there are 13 sts. Decrease at each end of following 4th row, following 3rd row and next alt row (7 sts). Work 1 row, then decrease 1 st at each end of the next 2 rows (3 sts).
Next row: Sl1, k2tog, psso. Fasten off.

For striped version, work as above, changing colour every two rows.

Heart motif

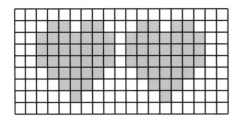

☐ A

▨ B

TO MAKE UP THE BALL

Darn in all loose ends. Mattress stitch pieces together alternating the striped and plain, or motif and plain sections. Leave one seam open for inserting stuffing. Stuff, then close the last seam.

Nursery Blocks

Keep toddlers happy with these pretty nursery blocks. They are knitted with motifs, interesting textures, and a variety of colours.

MATERIALS
Block with hearts:
50g balls of 4ply (sport-weight)
100% cotton: 1 x white (A),
1 x sky blue (B), 1 x lilac and
1 x muted green (C)

Blocks with anchors:
50g balls of 4ply (sport-weight) 100% cotton: 1 x white,
1 x light brown and
1 x sky blue
3mm (US: 2) needles
Toy stuffing
Bell(s) (optional)

TENSION (GAUGE)
23 sts and 32 rows to 10cm (4in) measured over st st on 3mm (US: 2) needles.

NOTE
Each block is made up of 6 squares and requires approx. 50g of yarn.

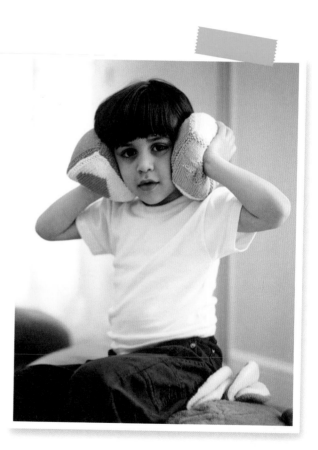

Anchor motif

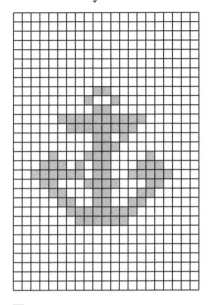

Heart motif

☐   K on RS, p on WS

⬜   P on RS, k on WS

☐   A

⬜   B

⬜   C

PLAIN OR HEART SQUARE

Cast on 27 sts and work 3 rows in moss st (seed st).

Next row: Keeping a border of 3 moss sts (seed st) on either side, work 30 rows in st st.

(Insert heart motif in centre if required – follow chart: work 4 sts, set motif 19 sts, work 4 sts.)

Work 3 rows in moss st (seed st). Cast (bind) off.

TO MAKE UP NURSERY BLOCK

Darn in all ends. Join all squares using mattress stitch, leaving small opening for stuffing. Insert bell if required, at this stage. Stuff, then close the seam.

Finger Puppets

Children can create their own productions with these finger puppets. They will encourage imaginative play and give hours of pleasure. Once you've mastered the simple pattern for the basic body, and have tried the octopus and mouse, delight and amuse your children by devising your own creatures to add to the cast.

MATERIALS
Oddments of 4ply (sport-weight) 100% cotton in sky blue (A), mid-blue (B) and cream (C)
3mm (US: 2) needles
Toy stuffing

TENSION (GAUGE)
23 sts and 32 rows to 10cm (4in) measured over st st on 3mm (US: 2) needles.

BASIC BODY
Cast on 15 sts.
Knit 2 rows.
Cont in st st, beg with a k row, until work measures 6cm (2½in) from cast-on; end on a p row *.
Next row: Shape top: (K1, k2tog), rep to end (10 sts).
Next row: P.
Next row: (K2tog) to end (5 sts).

Break yarn and draw through rem sts. Fasten off and join seam.

Octopus

BODY
Using yarn A, follow instructions for Basic Body to *.
Next row (make head): K1, * make 1, k1, rep from * to end of row (29 sts).
Work 11 rows in moss st (seed st).
Next row: K1, * k2tog, rep from * to end (15 sts).
Next row: P.
Next row: K1, * k2tog, rep from * to end (8 sts).
Break yarn and draw through rem sts. Fasten off.

LEGS (make 8)
Using yarn B, cast on 5 sts.

Cont in st st until work measures 7cm (2¾in).
Cast (bind) off.

TO MAKE UP THE OCTOPUS

Darn in all loose ends.
Join main seam on head and body piece, stuff head section. With running stitch, sew around bottom of head and draw up and secure (enclosing stuffing). Attach legs evenly around the body at the bottom of the head. Embroider smiley face as illustrated.

Mouse

BODY

Using yarn C, follow instructions for Basic Body.

TAIL

Using cream yarn, cast on 5 sts. Work in st st for 11cm (4¼in).
Next row: K2tog, k1, k2tog (3 sts).
Next row: P.

Next row: K3tog.
Cast (bind) off.
Pull work slightly – this allows it to coil into a roll.

EARS (make 2)

Using yarn C, cast on 4 sts.
Work 2 rows in st st.
Next row: Cont in st st, increasing 1 st at each end of this and every alt row, until there are 14 sts.
Work a further 3 rows without shaping.
Next row: Decrease 1 st at each end of this and every following row until there are 2 sts.
Next row: K2tog, fasten off.

TO MAKE UP MOUSE

Darn in all loose ends. Attach tail and ears. Embroider face and whiskers as illustrated.

Cat's Pyjamas Case

Tuck your pyjamas safely away and this smiley cat will keep it warm. She likes to laze on the bed all day and be close at hand for last-minute cuddles before bedtime.

MATERIALS
50g balls of DK (light worsted) cotton and acrylic blend: 2 x gold
Black embroidery thread for eyes and mouth
4.5mm (US: 7) needles
Remnant of fabric: 70 x 60cm (27½ x 23½in)
Lining (optional): 70 x 60cm (27½ x 23½in)
1m (39½in) length of ribbon to decorate
Toy stuffing

TENSION (GAUGE)
18 sts and 25 rows to 10cm (4in) measured over st st on 4.5mm (US: 7) needles.

HEAD – SIDES (make 2 pieces)
Cast on 17 sts and work 6 rows in garter st.
Next row: Increase 1 st at beg of row, k to end (18 sts).
Next row: K to last st, increase in last st (19 sts).

Next row: Cast on 7 sts, k to end (26 sts).
Work 5 rows without shaping.
Next row: K to last st, increase in last st (27 sts).
Work 7 rows without shaping.
Next row: K2tog, k to end (26 sts).
Next row: K to last 2 sts, k2tog (25 sts).
Rep last 2 rows six times (19 sts).
Work 1 row.
Next row: K to last 2 sts, k2tog (18 sts).
Next row: K2tog, k to last 2 sts, k2tog (16 sts).
Work 1 row.
Rep last 2 rows twice (12 sts).
Cast (bind) off.

HEAD – GUSSET
Starting at nose, cast on 2 sts.
Knit 1 row.
Next row: Increase 1 st at each end of row (4 sts).
Rep last 2 rows four times (12 sts).
Work 2 rows.
Next row: Increase 1 st at each end of

row (14 sts).

Rep last 3 rows four times (22 sts).

Work 16 rows without shaping.

Next row: K2tog, k to last 2 sts, k2tog (20 sts).

Work 3 rows.

Next row: K2tog, k to last 2 sts, k2tog (18 sts).

Rep last 4 rows six times (6 sts).

Cast (bind) off.

EARS (make 4 pieces)

Cast on 3 sts.

Work 2 rows.

Next row: Increase 1 st at each end of row (5 sts).

Rep last 3 rows until there are 17 sts.

Work 2 rows without further shaping.

Cast (bind) off.

TO MAKE UP PYJAMAS CASE

Sew the gusset between the two sides of the head, starting at the nose. Join the two side sections under the nose to the chin, leaving the neck open. Stuff firmly. Close the neck by sewing with running stitch and gathering the work; secure tightly. Embroider the eyes, nose, mouth and whisker features as illustrated. Sew each pair of ear pieces together, then attach to the head, gathering the wide edge slightly.

BAG

Lay out the fabric, wrong side up, and fold a hem along each 70cm (27½in) edge. Sew in place. With right sides together, put the newly hemmed edges together and sew, leaving an opening of about 20–25cm (8–10in) in the middle of the seam. Sew the bottom of the bag together, ensuring that the open seam is in the middle of the bag (not on the side). Insert a lining at this stage if required, using the same method, securing it in each of the two bottom corners, and sewing together at the opening. Make a hem on the top of the bag and sew. Gather the whole top of the bag using running stitch, ensuring that the cat's head fits neatly into it. Tack the head in place, with the opening at the back, and sew. Add ribbon to decorate.

Acknowledgements

Thank you Mum for your endless support and countless hours of patient knitting and for teaching me the craft so many years ago; I will always be grateful. Thank you Dad for my wonderful suppers and for the continual supply of tea. A huge thank you must go to my family and friends who encouraged me throughout this project and kept me going – I couldn't have done it without you!

I would like to thank Kate Buller at Rowan Yarns for supporting me over the years and Rowan for supplying the beautiful yarns. Thank you to Collins & Brown for the opportunity to make this book possible and in particular to Marie Clayton for your enthusiasm. To all the ladies who have spent time with me and who have supported me at my workshops over the years, I thank you too!

My final words of gratitude go to my partner Chris, who has been a tower of strength throughout this long process.

Picture credits
Cover photography by Rachel Whiting
Photography by Mark Winwood and John Garland